The Hour of the Wolf

The Hour of the Wolf

Gary Morris

All poetry @ The Estate of Gary Morris 2011.

Book organised and edited by Andy N.

Special thanks to Amanda for her help.

All rights are reserved. No reproduction, copy or transmission of this publication may be made without written permission.

The estate of the author have asserted their rights to be identified as the author of this work in accordance with the Copyright, Designs and Patents act 1988.

Published and printed by N Press, Stretford, Manchester.

Contents

(Introduction by Andy N)	Page 9
(Introduction by Gary)	Page 13
The Hour of the Wolf	Page 15
Dorothy	Page 16
Caravans	Page 17
Danger	Page 18
Desert	Page 19
Gardner's World	Page 20
Ghosts	Page 21
A Christmas Tale	Page 22
Whether Forecast	Page 26
These were my mothers	Page 27
No Hard Feelings	Page 28
Heroes back to save the day	Page 29
Calendar Fay	Page 30
Chav Generation	Page 33
Change	Page 34
Mystery Shopper	Page 35

Told you so	**Page 36**
Toni (Gary's story, a monologue)	**Page 37**
D.I.Y.	**Page 40**
Identity (Sing)	**Page 41**
Let's talk about Sex	**Page 42**
A Nice place to visit	**Page 43**
I don't do cathartic	**Page 44**
Morning	**Page 45**
Broadband - A Social Disease	**Page 46**
The Good Old Days (Short Play)	**Page 47**
Gothic Love	**Page 49**
Surprise	**Page 50**
Christmas Cheer	**Page 51**
Weeping Angels	**Page 52**
Yuletide	**Page 53**
Trenches	**Page 54**
Tears for heaven	**Page 55**
A Fine Situation	**Page 56**
Our son	**Page 60**
D'ya know	**Page 61**

Happy Anniversary	**Page 62**
Blood	**Page 63**
Transport	**Page 64**
Rainbow	**Page 65**
Bathtime	**Page 66**
Red Riding Bint	**Page 67**
Uniform	**Page 68**
Pub Menu	**Page 69**
A Winters Night	**Page 73**

Introduction..

To cut a long story short, when I left university in 2001, to say it was soul destroying in that last term and almost put me off writing poetry for good was a understatement and almost put off me writing altogether.

Fast-forward a few years to the end of 2003 and a friend of mine, Heather from my university days took over running and organising a creative writing group at Bolton University Library every Saturday morning and decided I must attend the group to get me back into writing.

The only problem was it started at 10am, and I lived and still live in Stretford which meant I would have to get up at 8am in the morning to make sure I get there in time, which during that stage in my life was a impossibility considering I was out until 2am or 3am most Saturday mornings.

Eventually, she managed to persuade me to go along – around the time of March 2004, and at that, I met Carole, another lady I used to go to university with and through her and Heather I met Gary, whose collection you now hold in your hands.

After Heather's group finished, the four of us joined another creative writing workshop called Haulgh Writers (later 24 Hour Arty People), and a few years after that group finished at the end of 2007, me, Gary and his partner Amanda formed Trio Writers, our own creative writing discussion group which then got a side project of a open mike night going too called 'Poets and..', which is a book itself that needs telling - both of which ran until Gary's untimely death in February 2010.

Looking back at this collection, I can remember some of these poems been wrote in workshops and in some cases been performed live in completely different versions – 'Gothic Love' which went through lots of constant re-drafting over a number of years or 'Surprise' which was a comedy poem wrote about a elderly lady who was ran over by a 62 bus, which when down poorly at a night was because a elderly lady that most of the audience knew had been ran down by a 62 bus a few weeks before and killed.

Comedy was certainly a major part of Gary's writing right from when I first met him in 2004 with a number of pieces which I am sure were wrote to shock and challenge audiences or 'No hard feelings' which if you look it originally, you would think it was a sympatric piece to an ex, but when you look at it more carefully, you can see something a totally different meaning in it.

Like my own work, Gary's work developed further over 2008 and 2009 when both of us used to perform poetry live and through our work in Trio Writers, where I started to develop stories within my poems instead of gags, and Gary's went into darker and deeper textures like paintings with words which I think was in part of his growing influence of the artist Victoria Francis in which he produced pieces such as 'Tears for Heaven' which is a rare piece of beauty which says so much in so few lines:

> *I hugged a dying angel,*
> *Her tears washed away my sin.*
> *"I've had enough of this life,"*
> *She told me.*
> *"No matter what I do it's not enough.*
> *"Mankind is split. Potential in conflict*
> *"Love and life corrupted hurts."*
> *I held her and cried,*
> *My tears baptising her.*
> *Stroking her head.*
> *"Thank you," she said.*
> *Then she was gone.*

Gary like I said before sadly left us at the beginning of 2010, and at his funeral and left a large archive of work from which this barely touches the tip of the iceberg.

Pieces like 'Caravans' is a nice contrast to the comedy pieces and the untitled piece with his own sense of energy of a small holiday in Cornwall with his family and then young nieces

> *' So much planned,*
> *So much to do and see.*
> *I used to have an itinerary*
> *But the twins coloured it in'*

At his funeral, I can remember the priest reading a incredibly beautiful poem which I had had never heard before called 'A Winter's night' which brought out a few lumps as it almost felt like he had wrote that on his death bed, which was then contrasted with his music before he went to the flames of the Laurel and Hardy theme tune, which in a way I guess summed him up .

And I hope he likes this short sampling of his work.

Andy N

At Home, September 2011

Andy N is a poet and writer based in Manchester, UK. He brought out his first book on N Press in 2010 'Return to Kemptown' and then followed it up with a split book with Jeff Dawson 'A Means to an End' through N Press and Half Evil Books in 2011.

He is currently working on his second full-length book 'The End of Summer'.

Introduction by Gary..

I'm a youthful 40-something (I love self delusion). I've enjoyed writing since I was a child. When I was in junior school I knew I could write better stories than Jane and Peter. Of course life decides it has other plans so my writing became something just for me.
After several relationships and a marriage I saw a leaflet in Bolton library about a writing group. I started going to that one and realised that everything people say about joining writing groups was true and when this one stopped I started going to another. Through feedback I refined my style and even managed to get a couple published in anthologies. I've been told I have a particular style but I don't know if that's good or bad. Did I also mention that I am the Master of the Universe.

(Wrote in 2006 by Gary for introduction to sample of work
On 24 hour arty people website)

The Hour of the Wolf

The Hour of the Wolf,
That's what they call it;
The time in the early hours of the morning
When your fears and anxieties
Manifest themselves in dreams and thoughts,
And your past reaches out of the darkness
To take hold and pull you back
Into your secret nightmare

Time slows down in the purgatory hours
And every thought shapes itself from the essence
Of agony and laughter that is your own sound.
So now I'm sat here,
Enshrouded in the diasporic maze of memories,
Feeling weary and drowning in darkness
But unable to sleep.
Feeling heavy in my heart but unable to stop the beat.
A tome of past voices chains me to then.

I'm feeling trapped, unable to escape
From the shadows of my self constructed room.

The Hour of the Wolf:
It has me by the throat.

Dorothy

(sing and skip) 'Lions and tigers and bears, oh my'
(sing and skip) 'Lions and tigers and bears, oh my'
SHUT UP YOU DAFT BITCH
Your not in Kansas anymore,
And while we're at it Toto is a mongrel,
The wicked witch isn't dead
She's morphed into a government
Taking away freedom and choice.
But that's ok 'cos the Wizard of Oz
Will rescue us won't he?
Get real you deluded cow,
What drugs are you taking these days?
For tin man read crack pipe,
For scarecrow read bag head,
For the lion think about a dealer.
Flying monkeys - too many mushrooms.
A yellow brick road full of dog shit,
Discarded needles, empty pop bottles, vomit, piss and kebabs.
Munchkins with ASBO's drinking White Lightning
All tooled up for a mugging.
The Emerald City in disrepair,
Run by corruption
Bang the heels on your fake designer shoes,
You still won't get to Kansas,
You live here now.

I once lived at the end of a rainbow,
Vibrant colours mixed with the pastel shades
Of a blurred vision of memories.
Red, orange, yellow, green, blue indigo, violet
A spectrum to cover all aspects of my life,
And amidst all this
I found no pot of gold,
Instead I found you
Much more precious.

Caravans

Sun, sea, Sangria.
Well ok, sun, sea, Scrumpy.
Mid-summer in Cornwall
A heat wave in full flow.
A perfect time to have a caravan holiday
With girlfriend, parents
And 2 five year old twin nieces.
So much planned,
So much to do and see.
I used to have an itinerary
But the twins coloured it in.

Danger

Have you ever wanted to be in a war zone ?
That's danger.
Have you ever made a pass at a friend's girlfriend ?
That's danger.
Have you ever confronted a group of drunken chavs ?
That's danger.
Have you ever driven over 100mph on a motorway
In the rain ?
That's danger (and stupid).
Have you ever had sexual thoughts about your mother?
That's just plain dodgy

Desert

Dehydration of my spirit,
A curse of emotion,
Being sucked dry by
The desert that's you.
I give you all I have
And receive nothing in return.
Desiccation of my heart
With no oasis in sight.
I saw your love once,
But now it's all dried up
And all I want to do
Is drink you again.

Gardner's World

"Hail Grimmerdhore! Forest of the One forest! Freehome and root, and preserver of the life sap of wood! Let the earthpower flow through this land."

"What?" I said.

"You heard: Hail Grimmerdhore! Forest of…"

I interrupted waving my hand. "I heard what you said, I just don't know what it means."
"It's fairly obvious," Philip sounded shirty, "I'm acknowledging the power of nature," he said, "the magnificence of the land and its ability to heal and repair itself when man has gouged his viciousness into the yielding flesh of our beloved planet." His eyes were wild and the sweat of a zealot ran down his face. He started again,"Ha-man rual tayba-sah carab ho-heeal," he said.

"We work in a garden centre you tit," I said.

Ghosts

I went for an early morning walk
Among the dead,
Birdsong touching each stone bed
Like an angel's kiss.

Grass was covered with the icy crust
Of forgotten souls, melting into the earth
As the first heat of a winter's sun creeps
Through the haze of the corpses' breath.

I tried to remember all of your names
By saying them out loud,
But your silent voices deafened me
And tried to pull me down.

Now I only have memories of some of you
The rest remain buried.
Echoes of life and death
Haunting me like the ghosts of a past
That isn't mine.

A Christmas Tale

"They're WHAT?"

"They're on strike."

"They can't be. It's impossible."

Mrs Claus shook her head, "come and see the impossible then," she said. Her husband, Santa, jumped up from his tinsel covered throne. His jolly red coat snagged on something as he stomped through the doorway. He tugged and the coat ripped.

"And get rid of this bloody holly and ivy, I'm sodding fed up with it, it gets everywhere, "he bellowed.

Mrs Claus loved her husband but he was so thick. After all, any normal person would go through a door if they had to deliver a parcel, but not Santa. No, he had to be different and do it the hard way by coming down the chimney. Mrs Claus blushed as she remembered a joke told to her by one of Santa's Little Helpers. She then began to chuckle to herself, the new houses with no chimneys really had him stumped at first, and he still hadn't told her how he managed to get past all those security systems. "Trade secret," he told her when she had asked. His acquaintance with Chris the dwarf was likely to yield more of an answer than any trade magazine. The other thing she worried about was his drinking. It was only a matter of time before he fell off a roof or was arrested for being drunk in charge of a sleigh. She could never understand why he insisted on drinking all those glasses of sherry, especially when he kept saying that he didn't like the stuff. Apart from the inconvenience of not having a convenience on the sleigh, it was dangerous. Mrs Claus had lost count of the number of times he'd crashed into a telephone wire. And if people could see what he'd written in the snow on their roofs they'd think twice about leaving drinks out for him.

"Itssh tradisshun-hic," he kept telling her. But no matter how hard she tried she could never figure out who had started the tradition. She pulled the secateurs from her festive apron, sighed and began to prune the doorway.

There was no background hum, the floorboards didn't vibrate. A bad sign. Santa tried to look on the bright side, "HO HO HO," he tried. Nope it didn't work. The sense of a fan and something hitting it would not go away.

The workshops were silent when Santa entered. At first he couldn't see anybody then he realised that gathered at the far end of the hangar sized workshop was the sea of green that were his pixie and elven workers – Santa's Little Helpers. It took a moment before he realised they were all looking at him. He felt intimidated but he was still the boss.
"GET BACK TO WORK, WE'VE GOT A DEADLINE TO MEET," he shouted down the room. He waited five minutes for the echo to die down and was just about to shout again when he noticed the green tide coming towards him, led by a pixie. They trekked towards Santa, the bells on their hats and shoes jingling in a threatening manner, they sounded to him like slay bells. Santa shivered. Santa's Little Helpers stood cutely in front of the jolly red giant. The lead pixie cleared its throat, its rosy red cheeks throbbing, and spoke. It had a microphone clipped to its cute little green tunic and its first words became a banshee scream escaping from the tannoy system. Everyone rammed their fingers in their ears except Santa. He was determined to show that he was in charge. The pixie adjusted the volume on the microphone.
"Oops," he, or it may have been a she, said. Santa could see its mouth moving but the ringing in his ears took time to fade away. He was not amused. The pixie felt intimidated but taking a deep breath started to speak slowly, one hand on the volume control, "I have been chosen by the brothers…"

"And sisters," a voice came from the crowd behind the pixie, who turned to acknowledge the speaker then continued.
"I have been chosen by the brothers and sisters to act as their spokes-pixie in this matter." Santa said nothing, just stood open mouthed, so the pixie went on. "The newly formed Union of Pixies, Elves and Faery Workers (manual and clerical) or UPEFW, as we are to be known, has decided to campaign for better working conditions. In short, with no offence to our members who are vertically challenged, we want a better deal." The pixie folded its arms.

"THE WHAT HAS DECIDED TO WHAT," Santa screeched as he comprehended what the pixie had just said. Santa's face went the colour of his jolly red jacket. "Get back to work you short arsed idiots before I crack some heads."

The pixie stood his ground, although if it were known his confidence had long since gone the way of a snowflake in a heat wave. When Santa had finished his ranting the pixie said,

"Those statements indicate extreme prejudice and are obviously sizeist, racist, and sexist and are slanderous – everyone in here has married parents. Listen Santa we don't want to cause trouble but we're a bit fed up of your attitude towards us. We spend half of the year making toys for you, which brings up the question of IT training, and the other half of the year wrapping the damn things up, and what thanks do we get? In a word sod all. We don't get any wages and we're all completely fed up of wearing green costumes with bells sown on them," the pixie was on a roll, "I think I speak for all the members when I say that we feel, look and sound like a load of pratts." There was a general murmur of agreement from behind the pixie.

"But you're only mythological constructs perpetuated in your present form as a sort of child control mechanism," said Santa. This made the pixie angry.

"Try telling the faerry on top of the Christmas tree that he, or she, is a mythological construct. How would you like to have a tree rammed up your...."

Santa held up his hand, "Okay, I get the idea. But look at it from my point of view. I have to go around the world on a dodgy sleigh, being pulled by reindeer that are way past their sell by and use by dates, delivering presents to every house in the world – not forgetting the time zones – including those with no chimneys. I have to do this all in one night. On top of this I am obliged to drink any sherry and eat any mince pies that are left out for me. The reindeers hate carrots. Dasher's favourite is a vindaloo curry and you can imagine what that's like for me because his arse is the one I see when I'm driving. And I hate sherry," nobody challenged him on this point," and mince..." the words were left unsaid, everyone in the room knew about mince pies. Tears were in his eyes, "I have to live in the coldest place on Earth and to top it all I have to wear this stupid jolly red suit and can't even have a shave." He tugged at his beard and broke down completely. His sobbing was the loudest noise in the building as everyone stared at him. Santa sat on the floor with his head in his hands.

The pixie patted Santa on top of his head then went back to the crowd of workers. After a brief discussion the pixie came to where Santa was sitting, a broken man staring at his future at the job centre.
"Santa we'll go back to work if you'll agree to our terms."
Santa looked up, hope in his eyes, "go on," he said.

"Well first," the pixie began, "we want some form of heating in the workshops." Santa nodded. "Then a lunch break of at least thirty minutes," another nod. "We want Rudolph to keep out of this building when we're working. He comes in giving orders, telling everyone he is Santa's chosen one, harassing the female staff, telling them what he'd like to do with his red nose. It's not very nice, especially when it starts flashing."

Santa nodded again, "and is there anything else?"
The pixie nodded, "just one more thing. You know how dangerous it can get around here, especially during the run up to Christmas and just after when we get the returned gifts. There's always someone getting injured, and then there's normal illnesses, etc"

"What do you want?" Santa's exasperation was clearly evident.

The pixie spoke quickly, "we want some medical provision to cover your workers all over the world. We want an Elf Service."

Santa thought for a moment, "okay but we'll have to get your people to meet my people to work out the details." A cheer went up through the workshop. The pixie raised its hand and called for silence.

"Before we start back to work how about a drink Santa, to celebrate our new working relationship?" Santa agreed. A glass of milk was passed to him. He stared at it, confused.

"Sorry Santa but as mythological stereotypes we can only drink milk."

"Bugger that," said Santa and pulled a bottle of vodka from under his beard. Unscrewing the cap he lifted the bottle," good elf everybody."
And they all drank heartily until the early hours of the morning. Their little bells jingling with happy tunes once more.

Whether Forecast

Lightning flashes,

A slow grumble in the sky.

Black clouds steal in from the north,

Boiling like hot oil

Threatening to pour onto the land

And drench a corrupt world in shadow.

An amorphous skin of nothing

Removing identity and detail.

Everyone becoming the same,

Spluttering words with no meaning

It's started to rain,

And I don't know whether to use an umbrella.

These were my Mother's

These were my mother's ,
She said she'd always look after me,
Now I guess she can.
She loved me,
I know she did,
All my life she was there,
Watching over me,
Protecting me,
Stopping me from making mistakes.
Like that time with Jean
From the garage.
Mum made me realise
That Jean was only after one thing.
So I stopped that.
Jean wasn't happy.
Mum was pleased,
She said I was a good boy.
Then there was dad.
He used to hurt both of us
And when I made him go away
Mum was sad at first,
But then she became very happy.
Every time I saw her she was smiling at me,
I guess I knew then that she would always
Be there for me.
So you can imagine my surprise
When she told me she would have to go away.
She said it was cancer,
But I knew she just wanted to be
On her own without me – I'd always suspected it.
But she'd promised to look after me,
And I couldn't let her break her promise.
So just before she went to Jesus she gave them to me.
She moaned at first but then let me have them.
Now she can always make sure I'm ok.
My mother always had beautiful blue eyes,
Now they're mine.

No Hard Feelings

Going away was something you always said you'd do
Even I can't remember
The number of times you threatened to leave but never did
So now I guess it's "goodbye" for good,
Time for both of us to move on.
Upsetting each other was never planned,
Friendship something we'd always have.
Feelings of love have long since departed and now even the
Echoes of our first times together
Dissolve in the dusk with the setting of the sun.
Beginning again is going to be hard for both of us,
I know we'll cope, we always have.
Time is supposed to be the great healer but
Choosing which clock to watch is always a problem. I know
Happiness will find us again. Until then no hard feelings.

Heroes back to save the day

Superman was my hero,
Then I noticed he had his underpants on the outside.
Retard I thought.
Then Batman became my hero,
But I noticed he wore a mask,
And had a young boy as a sidekick,
Perverted and disfigured, I thought.
Then there was Spiderman,
A bloke in lycra, wearing a gimp mask,
Fond of swinging,
S&M in groups, I thought.
I was fucked when it came to the X-Men and the Fantastic Four.

Calendar Fay

January

I am a new year.
The blood of the old year
Pooling on my breasts
Like Nature's milk,
Embracing my crimson corpse.

February

I am asleep, dreaming
Of what could have been -
What is -
And what may be.
My tears come easily.

March

I am the dark faerry.
My wings unused.
Flowers are dying in my hair
And I'm wearing shadows like a mantle.
My tears are red and my time is done.

April

Come to me for I am rebirth.
I am awakening, emerging from darkness,
All around me grows.
See my eyes. See my breasts
Then let my passion kill you.

May

Can you feel the bite of my teeth,
Your flesh yields to me,
Your blood feeds me,
Your soul yearns for me - I'll take it from you.
I am beauty - I'm the last you'll see.

June

This is my time.
I am the transition between life and death,
The light in the dark.
Among all the ghosts you know
I am the guide.

July

Your lips cry blood
When I kiss them.
Gaia hides us from the universe.
Sleep well my lover,
We are safe.

August

Dying eyes wandering among the dead,
Stone reminders of life and buried memories,
Caressed by a rustle of leaves.
Your lacrimosal gifts
Are feeding a dead Earth.
Your heart already rotted.

September

Lilith is my name
And I watch you - remembering my own grief.
I see your pain,
I see how you die a little each day.
Eden has gone, its' walls decayed and collapsed.
I cry for you.

October

My lights dim
And the abyssal darkness draws closer,
Stroking you with deceptive affection.
See my world, see my tears,
See my corpse.

November

You have no power to stop extinction.
See my anger emerging,
My corpse continuing to fight Charon.
No journey for me tonight,
See my neck, see my pulse.
Now it's your turn.

December

I am that which you dread,
Wearing a masque so you don't know me.
An eternal city of darkness awaits you,
Covered in the blood of condemned innocents.
I am Death.

Chav Generation

Burberry bastards in baseball caps and Burberry chic,
Hoodies colour co-ordinated with tracksuit bottoms tucked
Into socks, tucked into copies
Of expensive trainers,
Pink tracksuits with matching inanity,
The symbols of a chav generation.
A carpet-carrying gait,
MP3 players volumed to the max,
Lots of bling, half sovereign rings,
The symbols of a chav generation.

WKD, vodka or cider, maybe even Lambrini.
Hanging around in groups,
Intimidation, a lack of education,
The symbols of a chav generation.

Taking out frustration and angst
On phone boxes, bus stops and park benches.
Mouthing off to parents and authority,
"It's not my fault I'm a twat" a whine,
The symbols of a chav generation.

Vickie pollard type scowls and grunts,
"Am I bovvered,
"Yeah whatever"
Grandma at 30
ASBOS by the dozen
The symbols of a chav generation

Personally I'd shoot the fucking lot of them.

Change

I decided that I needed a change
So I went for a walk in the dawn
And saw Aurora's tear roll down a leaf and accept freedom
When it fell, taking me with it,
And for a moment I was a part of it,
Our confines reflected in each other's humour

The ice-cold breath from a waking Earth
Caressed my face and stroked my hair,
Its chill infiltrating the prison I wear.
Telling me that I'm not dead.

Passion's kiss crawled over the horizon
Reaching slowly towards me
Like blood seeping from a wound.
A wave of light turned into fingers
By the punctuation of the city,
And in spite of the warmth which
Rose in me like a lover's desire
I looked away.

I decided that I needed a change
So I went for a walk in the dawn
And all I saw was you.

Mystery Shopper

I used to be a mystery shopper
But then I got spotted.
Now I'm just an ordinary shopper
No mystery there.

Told you so

Told you my jokes and you smiled
I told you of my hopes and you wished me luck
I told you of my dreams and you said 'go on'
I told you of my shadows and you held out your hand
I told you of my sorrows and you dried my tears
I told you of my nightmares and you stroked my head
I told you of my loves and you embraced me
I told you of my soul and you made it complete.

Extract from 'Toni' (Gary's Story)

Looking around now, there are lots of faces here I don't know – except one. It was her best friend who told me – Toni never would have – too proud I guess. Speaking to my son for the first time was difficult but we managed.

Long silences, difficult sentences, unanswered questions – you know the drill. I think I told him about his mum – the one I remembered in any case. I don't know what he thinks, what he feels or even if he wants to keep in touch.

Looking at her picture now it's hard to believe she's the same Toni I met when I was almost 13. I don't even remember how we ended up together. I guess it was one of those 'sharing the same friends' things that you develop at school. She was a few years older than me and I could never understand why she wanted to go out with me, but she did.

Her eyes were beautiful, vibrant and full of life. They lit up when she smiled. She really was the proverbial ray of sunshine. I think we did 2 years together before we went our separate ways.

She was always ambitious and I remember when her best friend gave her a charm bracelet for her birthday, it had a Cross and, I think, a Saint Christopher on it.

She liked it because it came from her best friend. We were snogging on the church steps when she said,

"One day I'll get one of these and it will be platinum and full of diamonds." The future seemed so far away then.

She often told me of her plans and we spent hours sat on the back field while she talked about her future – not just her career but also her 'soul-mate' husband, the kids she'd have and their future. I was never mentioned.

She wanted her children to be happier than she was. Her father was a sociable man in public, but I'd heard things. Toni never said anything but I saw the bruises. She could normally hide them but when we were intimate (as much as awkward teenagers can be) I saw them. I didn't say anything – I didn't know what to say.

I once asked her if everything was ok. She told me things were fine and that she loved me, but those once beautiful, radiant eyes were now dead. We split up soon after.

I never really saw her after that, although I did bump into her a couple of times in town over the next 20 years.
The first time was fairly uncomfortable, but I had long ago realised that polite conversation is a good fall back for filling those strained moments.
"How are you Gary?" she asked.

"I'm fine. What are you up to these days?"

"Not a lot. Just started a job in a DIY shop."

"That sounds interesting," then silence. Nothing left to say to each other.

"Well I'd better be off."

"Yeah me too. Take care Toni. Good luck in your new job."

"Thanks Gary." Then she was gone. I watched her – she didn't look back.

The second time was only last year. She wasn't on her own though. They were coming out of a solicitor's office. She looked very smart in a grey pin stripe suit. She was stood next to an attractive, smart well-dressed man.

I was in my jeans and a t-shirt.

"Toni?" She was surprised at first, then she smiled and I saw the girl I first met.

"Hello Gary," the man she was with took hold of her right hand.

"John, this is Gary – he was my first boyfriend when I was 14. Gary, this is John my husband."

He smiled and gave her hand an 'affectionate' squeeze. Her fingers turned white and she flinched. I tried not to notice.

"I see you've done alright for yourself," I said.

"Yes, I'm an interior designer now. What about you?"

"I run my own business. Decided to take a day off and just chill for a bit,"

"It's alright when you can do that," he said and even though we all laughed there was hostility in his words.

"Any Kids yet Toni?" She was quiet and her eyes went red. It was one of those questions I wish I'd never asked. He looked angry.

"No... No kids," it was almost a whisper. I didn't know she was lying then – or was it simply a denial.

Lots of faces here I don't know – except one. It was her best friend who told me – Toni never would – too proud I guess.

Speaking to my son for the first time was difficult but we managed. Long silences, difficult sentences, unanswered questions – you know the drill.

I think I told him about his mum – the one I remembered in any case. I don't know what he thought, or if he wants to keep in touch.

"I think we need to be going now dear," John said to Toni. His eyes were dark. He started to pull at her but she pulled back. He wasn't happy. I looked at her and saw the desolation and regret of a girl I once loved and my heart died.

This time as she walked away she did look back.

"Goodbye Gary."

"Goodbye Toni"

D.I.Y

I'm sat in a room of four white walls,
Clean and sterile like a TV hospital.
They never used to be like this.

It wasn't too long ago that they had colour.
Passionate reds, happy yellows, loving greens.
The colours gradually became pale until
I painted over them in white:
And now they're just like me –
Blank and clean
No features I can see,
No emotions I can feel.

I'm sat in a room of four white walls,
And from the corner of my eyes
I can see where the white is thinnest –
And the colours bleed through

Identity (sing)

You are you,
I am me,
We've lost our identity,
And the men in suits
Still tell us what to do,
Do you ever get the feeling
You're in a political zoo?

Let's talk about sex

"Go on, you know you want to.

"Its been weeks since we had a good hard shag.

"I'll do foreplay if you want,"

I was sounding whiney.

"Yes I know it's dangerous

"We don't have to do foreplay, although

"A bit of oral is always a good start."

I tried not to sound too desperate.

I stroked her back.

She looked at me with the air of aloofness

She always showed me.

Then she turned away,

And in that special way said

"Baa."

A Nice Place to visit

I'd heard so many people talk about it,
That pilgrimage everyone seems to want to take,
To that special place
Where you can "find yourself"

"Don't get lost," I used to say.
I'd see some of them going on their journey
Luggage well packed,
Constantly checking their passports and visas.

I never had the urge to follow,
After all I've too much to do here
And I've got much better places to visit.

Then you left me.

        And as you passed into the
        Turned page of my life,
        I saw I had no choice –
        So I made the journey.

        And when I got there
        I saw it was glorious
        And it was almost as if, in spite of everyone else,
        I was the only person there.

        I stayed for a while, losing track of time whilst
        Guiltily indulging my hedonism,
        Revelling in the visceral pleasure of your absence,
        Tasting the salty residue of my swimming.

But all good things come to an end
And the pleasure turned to pain,
The smile to frowns,
The hopes to despair.
That's when I decided to leave.
Misery – a nice place to visit
But I wouldn't want to live there.

I don't do cathartic

I don't do cathartic,
I'd rather talk about the sea,
Ships and piers and salty chips,
An idyllic childhood,
Full of sunshine and happy memories.

Seagulls shitting,
Tourists littering,
Hen nights, stag nights
Everyone pissed and full of shite
Another wonderful seaside night.

I don't do cathartic,
I'd rather talk about me.

Morning

Darkness hides as the light
That destroyed Icarus
Rises above the horizon.

Early morning mist evaporates
And slowly the land breathes
And returns to life.

It's not long before colours return,
And the light retreats,
Gaia reclaiming her realm.

Pushing away the nightmares
And shadows that pervade an infertile life,
An illumination of desiccation.

Broadband – A Social Disease

Have you been Googled ?
Or even Googled yourself ? (shame on you),
Does your face fit on Facebook?
Have you seen yourself on YouTube?
Have you been hacked
Or infected by a Trojan?
Are you a blogger
With teraflops of data,
Stored on a collection of data sticks and memory cards?
"Spam, Spam, Spam, Spam"
Monty Python had it right.
What speed does your binary life run at?
Not forgetting it may run slower at peak times.
Is your web browser up to date,
MSN means Machines Serve No-one,
Can't you see it controlling your fate.
A remote control of convenience
Taking you where it wants you to go.
The server has become the master,
Update your firewall, and be careful of
People who talk about phishing
And the virus a way of life.
Don't let someone take your place on Myspace
Instead, let's talk and meet face-to-face.
So, have you ever been Googled?

The Good Old Days

A man in robes stands at the front of a wooden ship looking across a vast ocean. It's raining heavily and the wind is blowing. He seems lost in his own thoughts.

A woman, also in robes, comes up and stands next to him – he doesn't see her. They remain silent for a while, then she speaks.

Mrs Noah: Noah (he doesn't hear her)

Mrs Noah: NOAH (shouting)

He still doesn't hear so she pushes him and he nearly falls over.

Noah: What are you doing you stupid cow? I could've gone over the side

Mrs Noah: STOP COMPLAINING (shouting). I KNOW IT'S A BIG BOAT BUT..."

Noah: How many times do I have to tell you? It's a friggin' ark not a boat.

Mrs Noah: WHATEVER (still shouting) ANYWAY WHAT I WAS GOING TO SAY WAS...

The wind and rain suddenly stop, the sun comes out. Noah and his wife look around, then at each other.

Noah: I thought it'd never stop. Trouble is I've no idea where we are.

Mrs Noah: (exasperated) Great. I suppose we'll just have to keep on drifting.

Noah: (ranting) What is it with you woman? I tell you that God's told me to build and ark and you say 'Oh hearing voices now are we?' then you complain about me building it; 'that's a nice piece of wood I'd say', then you'd say 'don't you think we've got enough wood?'
Then it starts raining and all the animals start coming, the kids were happy and helping out and all you could say was 'don't expect me to clean up all their shit, and what about the noise?'
Then you complain that I didn't. put in an en-suite bathroom for us

Mrs Noah: (arms folded. Obviously used to these outbursts)

    'have you quite finished?

Noah: I've not even started.

Mrs Noah: Sorry you misunderstood. What I meant to say was (raised voice – not shouting) YOU ARE FINISHED

Noah shuts up and looks at his wife.

Noah: what can I do for you dear?

Mrs Noah: I was going to say, before you started acting like a baby (Noah lowers his head and starts shuffling his feet), that Shem opened a hatch to let in some fresh air and one of the doves got out.

Noah: Bugger, that's the last we'll see of that.

Gothic Love

A stygian fortress of infernal memories
Crouches silently behind us,
Its spectral turrets illuminated
By the sterile light of Selene.
The dead wings of the Abyss
Embrace our pallid carcasses with sensual finality
As the coolness of your fingers stroke my spine,
And the touch of corruption becomes my shroud.

Through my bones
I feel the slow beat of your heart
And succumb to its immortal fullness.
Blue blood veins stretch your flesh
And threaten to erupt with
The colour of shadows.
Like a vampire's kiss
The taste of love coats my lips and
I devour the exhilaration of your life,

Temptress eyes with the promise of undying seduction
Draw me in and
I am lost in the miasma of Underworld emotion
That is you.
Your voice wraps itself around me
And comforts the child within – no longer afraid of the night.
Your succubus breath intoxicates
And the confusion of desire is gone,
I bare my neck
And become a creature of yours
Once more.

Surprise

Your death came as a big surprise
Especially for you.
We hadn't known you were ill.
You kept it buried and
Didn't leave a map
No 'x' marks the spot or a
Trail of breadcrumbs for us to follow.

Looking back now you're gone
It seems like we missed those
Signs you did give us.
No longer hungry, always tired
Finding you weeping was a shock
"I'm just feeling a little down" you'd say
And shrug my arm off your shoulder.

Your aches and pains were managed by drugs
Which you locked away from us, and
We were worried about your drinking
But didn't want to cause a fuss
Your death came as a big surprise
When you were run over by the 62 bus.

Christmas cheer

It was my third Christmas alone,
The last two passed without incident
This one, however, was different.

This year (or is it last year) I was in my own place
This brings dilemmas specific to single people –
So I avoided them by going out.

My cardboard collection of friends
Was bigger than last year
But I still hung them on a piece of string.

Jason and the Argonauts
The Wizard of Oz
Decorations or none.
I couldn't decide on a real tree
Or a fake one.
If I choose a real one
I have the problem of tidying up
When its many branches fall apart.
If I choose a fake one
It will last forever and never fade,
But nothing about it will be real
Like my memories of us.
The falseness is that we grew apart
The reality is that we fell apart
That's why it hurt so much.
An elastic emotion that snapped
Under the strain.
You never fall up
You only ever fall down.

Weeping Angels

The first time I saw you became an experience in itself.
You walked into a room and everyone else disappeared.
All I could see was you and 'though you didn't notice me at first
I knew you could feel my presence.
Your first smile was a beacon, a bit like a lighthouse guiding the lost towards a safe port.
Now things have changed and what is has become what was,
A stone heart crying blood,
Eyes closed, darkness a preference to the light of reality,
Covered in ivy and hugging a weeping angel

Yuletide

T'was the night before Christmas,
And all through the house
Nothing was stirring, not even a small rodent.
My mother was remembering the ghost
Of all we used to have,
A disturbing fashion of memories with a knife,
Soaked in the pool of blood that is a families past.
Shimmering corpses dancing in
The crimson beat of repression and humiliation.
You thought you'd found a prince,
Instead you tripped over a frog.

Croak.

Trenches

Let me write a poem
That has miles not metres or feet,
I want to construct a quatrain
That rhymes or maybe it doesn't.

For you a haiku
Showing a form to arrange
Two stanzas are one.

I'll come and go through poetic hell
And eventually you'll come to know
The pain of a contrived villanelle.

How many tercets had bid farewell,
As the number will gradually grow
I'll come and go through poetic hell.
Would you like a lai
To brighten your day
Or not.

I don't think I'll bother with rhythm and meter
And stick to writing what suits me.
I'm not concerned about being Chaucer
And Shakespeare doesn't appeal.
I just want to be like the greatest of all,
The one whose words strike to the heart of the world.
I want to create like the man in the trenches
Covered in blood and gore,
Living in mud and death in the First World War.
He saw things as they really were
Amid the deaths' of a million sons.
I wish I could write a poem
As good as Baldric's "German Guns

Tears for heaven

I hugged a dying angel,
Her tears washed away my sin.
"I've had enough of this life,"
She told me.
"No matter what I do it's not enough.
"Mankind is split. Potential in conflict
"Love and life corrupted hurts."
I held her and cried,
My tears baptising her.
Stroking her head.
"Thank you," she said.
Then she was gone.

A Fine Situation

It wasn't long before Bo Peep discovered that she'd lost her flock. At first she panicked then started to think where they could have gone. She regretted her little afternoon session with Wee Willie Winkie. Then there was the little delay spent talking to her hoody mates, Little Red Riding, Little Boy Blue, Jack (magic beans he'd told her but the smiley faces printed on each one told a different story), and she tried not to think about that slut Little Miss Muffet (a naming theme going on here Peep thought). Peep ignored the rumours spread by the pig in the straw house about Incey Wincey Spider and his alleged bathroom activities with the Muff.

Then it struck her, the little boy down the lane was constantly asking about Bo Peep's sheep, and he was a devious bastard. Ever since he'd rustled the black one - which hadn't been seen since, although there were suggestions of strange noises in the night from down the lane – he'd shown an unhealthy interest in getting more. The Gingerbread Man said he was convinced that he was trying to start a Baarem.
The Three Bears, who lived next door to the Little Boy who lives down the Lane remained tight lipped. It was obvious that he had an enforcer intimidating potential witnesses. Little Red said she had seen the newcomer to the village spending a fair amount of time with the 3 Bears.

She thought her name was Goldilocks. Although it was known that the Big Bad Wolf would lean on people if he got the odd Granny or two. The Woodsman was still under arrest due to his activities with Sleeping Beauty – before she awoke. And though Beauty wasn't bringing charges it was felt that because the Handsome Prince was extremely angry with him that it was in his best interest to stay locked up.

Hansel and Gretel's ASBOs had expired and many thought it strange they disappeared the day after.

"Good riddance to them," some people said. There are those who think they went to torment the old lady in the middle of the forest. The Sheriff's men thought it strange that the two should buy several loaves of bread before they left though.

Bo Peep had a sneaking suspicion that the disappearance of her sheep had something to do with The Ugly Sisters and The Evil Stepmother, she'd seen them eating at a ball a few years ago.

Pinocchio walked past her in the street and smiled. She blushed, remembering the last time they'd met. She was still convinced that he'd tricked her into making him lie. Seeing him reminded her that she needed to speak to Geppetto and ask him to reshape the end of Pinocchio's nose.

Bo Peep didn't usually go down the lane so she was a little nervous, looking from side so side and behind her until she reached the Little Boys House.

She stood at the gate, hesitating and trying to summon the courage to go through.

A heavy tap on her shoulder made her jump. She turned and came face to face with a hard faced women. A recent scar ran down her left cheek, still bright red, and the tattoos on her arms merged into the bruised knuckles on each hand.

Her steel toecap boots looked worn and well used. The stained dungarees she wore looked old and encrusted with suspicious rust coloured marks. Her vest top was struggling to keep her breasts in. She also had curly yellow hair, which obviously hadn't been washed or combed for some time.

She took the cigarette out of her mouth and smiled at Bo Peep. Her tobacco stained teeth chipped in places, with a couple missing.

"Are you looking for something sweetheart ?" Her voice was like gravel being sifted through glass and Bo Peep shuddered imagining each word being shredded before it emerged wheezing, it's menace clawing and infiltrating any ear it touched.

"Well.....?" she asked again. Bo Peep was brought out of her reverie. "Well it's like this, I used to have a flock of sheep. Then they weren't there. Gingerbread mans said.... Well it doesn't matter what he said," she was rambling.

"Shush." Goldilocks put her nicotine stained finger on Bo Peep's lips. "We'll talk about the Gingerbread Man later, but for now – WHY ARE YOU HERE ?" Think about your answer."

"I just wanted to know if the Little Boy knew anything about my sheep." Goldilocks put her face close to Bo Peep's.

"He doesn't," she said. Stale tobacco breath washed over Bo. A figure emerged from the house wearing nothing but a towel around his waist; he coughed and spat out a mouthful of phlegm.
"What's going on Goldi?"

"Nothing I can't handle," she shouted over her shoulder.

Bo looked at the Little Boy. She looked him up and down and felt he hadn't been a little boy for some time.

Goldilocks grabbed Bo Peep and lifted her off her feet.

"Eyes off, he's spoken for. Look at him like that again and sheep will be the last thing on your mind, and the only thing you'll be looking for will be a good plastic surgeon – get my meaning?"

Bo Peep nodded. Goldilocks put her down and the Little boy went back inside but, as he was closing the door, Bo Peep caught a glimpse of something white and fluffy running around inside the house.

Goldilocks caught her look.

"You saw nothing, now just piss off and stop harassing us – I mean him." Bo Peep walked away, fuming. She had mates who would help. The Fairy Godmother owed her a favour, as did Puss in Boots and the Seven Dwarfs, and what she did for Cinderella definitely deserved a return favour.

There was a knock at the door, it was Mother Goose.

"Hello Bo, I have some information about your sheep."

The Three Blind Mice bodyguards surrounded the Goose. The fact that they couldn't see had fooled a lot of people over the years – the Cheshire Cat was testament to what they could do given the opportunity. He'd learned his lesson the hard way after he picked on the Doormouse. They 'reasoned' with him and he soon developed a nervous twitch when in the presence of any rodent.

Bo Peep had always been suspicious of Mother Goose and had tended to avoid her, but if she knew something about the sheep then she was prepared to listen.

"What information?" she asked.

The Goose laughed, "the information isn't free cutie."

Bo Peep knew there had to be a catch.

"What do you want Mother?"

"There's a boy called Jack. He lives at the other end of the village. It seems he had a little adventure not long ago which resulted in his acquisition of a special goose."

"What's so special about it?" Bo Peep asked.

"That's not important. All you need to know is that if you want the information you get me the goose," Mother Goose answered in a way that said 'don't ask any more questions'. "He normally leaves his bedroom window open. His mum's got dementia and you can find him down at the Cattle Market pub. He's the one at the end of the bar feeling guilty about killing the giant.

"But Jack's my friend. I can't break into his house. And what about his mum?"

"It's up to you. They're not my sheep. And as for his mum, she's three sheets to the wind, and is usually sedated when Jack goes out."

"But....," Bo Peep began but was interrupted By Mother Goose.

"Let me put it this way cutie, in a way that doesn't cause you too much brain work. This is not a request that has an optional element."

She nodded to the three blind mice, who ignored her. She sighed.

"Threatening posture please."

The mice started to squeak, waved their white sticks, and Bo Peep shivered when she saw her distorted reflection in their dark glasses. She wasn't so impressed by their guide fleas though.

Our son

Dear stranger,
We will never meet,
But the grave you stand before
Belongs to our son.
His picture is on the headstone.

Thank you for the time you take
To stand and read this,
And spend a moment with our son.
Please take a penny from the cup
And place gently on top of his stone.

For then we know he isn't forgotten,
And when you leave this place
You will take a piece of the love
We had for him
And it will become a part of your life,
As he is always a part of ours.

D'ya Know

D'ya know I really don't care about the state of the economy, U.K, European, or planetary. I don't care about global warming and I'm tired of hearing the constant bullshit produced by the bullshit machines most people call government. Honesty, integrity and tolerance – three words foreign to EVERY politician and psychotic militant.

If it doesn't bring them money, fame or kudos they're not interested – although I suspect money and power are the main driving factors: forget about the rest of the population who just want to live. So a child dies, a suicide bomber kills innocents, as long as the politicians and the fundamentalists line their pockets and think they're making a statement who gives a shit about the rest of the world.

"Out of touch with reality," how often have you heard that phrase, yet when you think of the people it's applied to how accurate is it when it's usually said by people who disagree with those who are "out of touch with reality."

Political sustainability relies on the individual trusting those who decide how they should live, die, believe and think – when those they trust forget about the individual, unless it's them of course.

Fatwahs and Papal Sees – all creations (with a small c) to direct people, to tell them what they think.

Could I say Jesus and Mohammed were gay lovers without getting lynched. I'm not allowed to think for myself because I may upset someone.

I've got news – tough shit.

Maybe Nietchze was right.

Still I do like fish fingers.

Happy Anniversary

An anniversary is a funny thing,
It's the knot we tie in time
To remind us of something important –
The birthday of an event
We sometimes want to forget.

An anniversary isn't just a day,
It's an eternity you can't ignore.
It's tattooed on your brain
And nailed to your heart.
A post-it note from life.

Some anniversaries are fatally drawn to
Each other and collide in a
Day of emotion –
Like two run away trains on the same track
Rushing towards each other.
You can feel the vibrations as they get
Closer, and close your eyes because you don't
Want to see them hit – but you always peek
And see that you're a passenger.
SMASH – you're a wreck.
A tangled mess of twisted emotions,
Distorted memories and limbless dreams.
You can't even be an innocent bystander.
You'd rather be sometime else,
But you know you'll catch the same trains next year –
And remember this year's crash.

If I ever meet the person who said
Happy anniversary,
I'll smack them in the mouth.
Anniversaries aren't happy,
They're just a way of living in the past
So you don't have to live in the present.
You carry your past into your future.
That's the thing about anniversaries –
Once you've got them they won't go away.
So have a Hallmark anniversary, sweet and twee.
Enjoy your day. Get a card covered in flowers and best wishes,
But don't get one for me.

Blood

"Let me see. Yes I have been out."

The tone of her voice chilled me. There was malice and a definite threat in her words, challenging me to go further. I declined the invitation. Her crimson lips shone in the moonlight and her black dress made her melt into a background of shadow.

"Have you nothing to say ?" she asked. A rustle of her dress brought her face to face with me. I'd never even noticed her movement.

I could see the hunger in her eyes and feel the blood flowing through my veins. I felt I was enticing her, almost begging her to take my life's blood. I took a step back – and a deep breath.

It seemed strange that I had been following her cautiously for many months and hadn't noticed her sensual beauty, and now I found myself in this situation only just noticing her.

She bared her teeth and screamed at me,
"I've found you out. I've discovered your hellish plots against me."

"You've still got to fill in your tax return," I said.

Transport

Red Lorry, Yellow Lorry,

Blood flowing, no need to worry.

A tongue-twisting, mind bending

Head fuck.

Politicians trying to distract you

By patting your head and

Rubbing their bellies.

You're placated,

They're sated on their lies and deceptions.

"I'm alright Jack,

"Vote for me Jack,

"I'm about to stab you in the back jack."

Red lorry, yellow lorry

Now a motorway pile-up.

Rainbow

Spectrum emotion in a ball of string
Love is yellow
Hate is red
Sadness is black
Hope is white.
What colour are you today?

Personally I'm yellow
With a hint of white and green
My redness a glow on the horizon.
And so-
Are you an emotional dusk
Or an emotional dawn.

I'm on a happy bus to pretty land,
And there are many spare seats.
Take my hand
And let me take you to the sunshine.

Bathtime

Have you ever looked at bubbles in a bath when you put your favourite foam in it. It's like a small universe. Each bubble is a galaxy – some bigger than others, colliding into each other and merging. Sometimes they become bigger, but most of the time they just pop.

Large ones. Small ones. All bubbles.

A bit like the memories we carry within ourselves.

Some are so huge that getting overwhelmed is inevitable. Others small enough not to be noticed, until they join with others, and before you know it small memories have crashed together and become a part of something much bigger that can't be ignored.
Tears, heartache and laughter all become a deluge of who you are.

A hand in the bath to give the water a stir and all the bubbles change.

Red Riding Bint

Once upon a time there was a cute little tooth fairy. She'd been around for a while but always looked after herself and she turned heads when she walked down the street on her days off, and it wasn't her teeth people were looking at . One day she came across a dead child drenched in the filth of a world of corruption. The child had no teeth – someone she'd missed. It was at that point she decided that taking bloodied teeth from under sleeping children's pillows wasn't a legitimate career, especially when those kids that woke up and saw her were psychologically damaged for the rest of their lives.

She discussed the options with her careers advisor (a mister Santa Claus) who decided a more gentle profession would be more apt. He gave her a red cloak and asked her to look after his granny.

Uniform

I hope you don't mind me saying but I think you're very pretty. What you're wearing suits you and you do have beautiful eyes.

I know you're probably not used to people saying like this to you – after al it's not the British way – but when you see someone who imprints themselves on your retina, your heart, your soul it's important to be honest about your feelings.

Sorry, what's that? You're not interested?

Fucking women traffic wardens.

Pub Menu

This little vignette is made all the more shocking, I suppose, because of the fact that I was stone cold sober when it happened last year.
My girlfriend of four weeks worked as a chef in one of those country pub-cum-restaurant places. My job was to pick her up after work which, due to the popularity of the place, invariably meant that I was stood waiting for her at the bar drinking coffee and talking to the landlord and other staff.

It was on one of these occasions when a woman came to the bar and interrupted the conversation I was having with Nigel, the landlord. She was with a party of people celebrating a 50th birthday. The party had been allocated a raised area of the pub that could be curtained off if needed. She asked Nigel if he could wear a silver wig and read a poem to the birthday girl.

Nigel refused immediately, citing age and girth as reasons why he couldn't do it.

"But Gary will do it," he volunteered me. I knew I'd be waiting another twenty minutes so I agreed. After all it was only reading a poem. So with a long silver wig, precisely placed, on my head and poem in hand I followed the woman to the birthday party.

There were about thirty people in the group, most at various stages on the drunkenness spectrum, talking and laughing. A few were looking at me with a certain amount of confusion on their faces.

"I'd like a bit of silence and the presence of the birthday girl at my side," I announced when I reached the centre of the group.

When I was sure everyone was looking at me with my arm around an attractive woman, I began to read the poem. Whilst I can't remember the words of the poem I do remember delivering the lines with a certain amount of gusto and passion. A few minutes later and it was over. I got a kiss off the birthday girl and a handshake off her husband. Then, just as I was about to leave the party a voice shouted out,

"Are you not going to strip then?" The group didn't go quiet but it did seem like it. I looked at the speaker, a very pretty blonde lady with a twinkle in her eyes. I smiled at her.

"I will if you will," I challenged, "every item I take off you take one off." She was silent. "I'll even give you a head start. Seeing as I'm wearing more than you I'll take my shoes and socks off." I assumed that the fact she was surrounded by her friends and family that she would back out, but I hadn't taken into account the alcohol.

"You're on." She stood in front of me.

"I'll give twenty quid to whoever takes the most off." It was the birthday girl's husband. He pulled the curtain across, cutting off the raised area from the rest of the pub.

I removed my shoes and socks as promised. "I'll go first," I said.

I took off my sweatshirt and put it neatly on a chair.

"Your turn."

"Get 'em off," the rest of the group urged us.

She took off her blouse to reveal a black silk cami-top underneath. The outline of her bra evident through the material.

"Go on then, if you're not chicken," she said.

Now I know that I haven't got an Adonis style physique but a challenge is a challenge. I pulled my t-shirt over my head, doing my best not to hold my stomach in.

"He's got a duck on his back," a voice shouted, referring to the heron tattoo on my shoulder.

"Let me look." My co-stripper turned me round. "Very artistic," she said, sensually scraping her nails over my back and sending a shiver throughout my body. A camera flashed.

"What are you taking off next?" I asked her. She turned me round so that we were facing each other again and took a step back. Then starting at her neck she ran her hands slowly down the front of her body until it reached the bottom of her cami-top. Our eyes never left each other. She raised the top inch by inch to reveal her holiday-tanned skin. Her semi-transparent bra showing off her figure and leaving nothing but imagination to the imagination.

I unfastened my belt then my jeans and pulled them over my feet, putting them with the rest of my clothes on the chair. Without hesitating she unfastened her skirt and let it slide over her thighs and fall to her feet. She stepped out of it and put her hands on her hips. The strobe effect of the camera flashes providing stop motion images that burned into my retina and my memory. Her matching thong having the same effect on me as her bra, I just hoped no-body noticed.

"You know the only way to win is to take both of them off," I said to her. My hands were in the waistband of my only remaining item of clothing and I was gently teasing them down. She carried on looking as my underwear got lower. Then several cameras flashed and, like being woken from a trance, she said,

"Ok you win. I can't take anything else off."

"Are you sure?"

"If you want to take it all off then go ahead," she said, "but I'm getting dressed."

"I guess we'll call it a draw then." I began to put my clothes back on. The birthday girl and her husband came over to me. He pressed a twenty-pound note into my hand.

"That was fantastic," he said, "you've certainly made it a memorable birthday party. Well done."

"I agree," said the birthday girl, "thanks for everything and making my birthday special." She kissed my cheek and whispered "although I must admit to wanting you to take it all off as you seemed to be enjoying things."

I blushed.

She smiled and went back to the party.

My stripping friend gave me a hug. "That was fun. I didn't think you'd go all the way,"

"a challenge is a challenge," I said.

"I must admit," she said, "I haven't been this turned on in a long time.

My husband's in for a busy night."

"Lucky husband," I said, "enjoy the rest of the party."

"I will now," She kissed and hugged me, and then I was alone again.
I pulled back the curtain and went back to my original space at the bar. My girlfriend was waiting for me.

"What have you been doing?" she wasn't happy.

"I've just been reading a poem and having a laugh with the birthday party," I answered in my defence.

"Why was the curtain drawn then, and what was all the noise?"

"People were enjoying themselves. What are you fussing about?"

I felt a tap on my shoulder. It was the birthday girl's husband. He had a digital camera in his hand – one of those where you can review your pictures.

"Is this your girlfriend?" he grinned.

"Oh shit," I thought.

A Winters Night

If on a winter's night,
You should think of me,
I ask but one thing,
That you remember
The springs we have spent together,
And how we reveled in the golden glory
Of the shoots of sunny days,
When daffodils shone,
And became more than flowers
When we were together.

As spring follows winter
Thus does summer follow spring.
When the verdant landscape
Embraces us, and trees bear fruit,
Life in abundance all around
Embracing us.
And hand in hand
We feel a connection with nature,
And each other.

Then does autumn follow summer,
And the rustle of the golden leaves
As we walk through them
Sounds like our hearts beating together,
Blessing the romance we have.

And now as the icy fingers of years end
Caress our faces,
Memories of what was and visions of what will be
Tantalize us with promises
Of a love undying.

I ask that when we are apart,
If on a winter's night,
You should think of me
Know that I am thinking of you.

www.ingramcontent.com/pod-product-compliance
Lightning Source LLC
Chambersburg PA
CBHW071413040426
42444CB00009B/2223